Chef's Choice: The Leading Cauliflower Cookbook

A Collection of Gourmet Cauliflower Recipes That Will Amaze You

BY: Valeria Ray

License Notes

A Special Reward for Purchasing My Book!

Thank you, cherished reader, for purchasing my book and taking the time to read it. As a special reward for your decision, I would like to offer a gift of free and discounted books directly to your inbox. All you need to do is fill in the box below with your email address and name to start getting amazing offers in the comfort of your own home. You will never miss an offer because a reminder will be sent to you. Never miss a deal and get great deals without having to leave the house! Subscribe now and start saving!

https://valeria-ray.gr8.com

Contents

Introduction

MMMMMMMMMMMMMMMMMMMMMMMMMMMMMMMMMMMM

Chapter I - Fresh and Delicious Cauliflower Salads

You really need to try all these delicious cauliflower salads we've gathered just for you! They taste and look wonderful!

MMMMMMMMMMMMMMMMMMMMMMMMMMMMMMMM

(1) Cauliflower Salad and Tahini Dressing

This is such a sweet combination! It's simply one of our favorite cauliflower salads!

Prep Time: 10 minutes

Total Cooking Time: 40 minutes

Serving Size: 4

List of Ingredients:

- 1 cauliflower, florets separated
- 2 Tbsp. olive oil
- 1 small red onion, sliced
- ½ bunch parsley, chopped
- Salt and black pepper to the taste
- 15 ounces canned chickpeas, drained
- ½ tsp. smoked paprika

For the salad dressing:

- 2 garlic cloves, minced
- ⅓ cup tahini paste
- ⅓ cup water
- ¼ cup lemon juice
- ½ tsp. cumin, ground
- Salt and black pepper to the taste

MMMMMMMMMMMMMMMMMMMMMMMMMMMMMMM

Instructions:

1. Arrange cauliflower florets on a lined baking sheet, add red onion, salt, pepper and oil, toss, roast in the oven at 400°F for 20 minutes, flip and roast for 10 minutes more.

2. Meanwhile, in your food processor, mix tahini with garlic, lemon juice, water, cumin salt and pepper and whisk well.

3. In a salad bowl, mix chickpeas with smoked paprika, parsley and cauliflower mix and toss.

4. Add salad dressing, toss well and serve.

Enjoy!

(2) Colored Cauliflower Salad

This looks amazing and it tastes so good!

Prep Time: 10 minutes

Total Cooking Time: 12 minutes

Serving Size: 16

List of Ingredients:

- 1 cauliflower head, florets separated
- 1 broccoli head, florets separated
- 1 yellow onion chopped
- 1 cup feta cheese, grated
- ½ cup bacon, cooked and crumbled
- 1 cup whip cream
- 1 tsp. mustard

MMMMMMMMMMMMMMMMMMMMMMMMMMMMMMMMMMM

Instructions:

1. Put cauliflower and broccoli florets into a pot, add the water to cover, bring to a simmer over medium heat, cook for 2 minutes, transfer to a bowl filled with ice water, leave aside for 1-2 minutes, drain and put in a large salad bowl.

2. Add onion, cheese and bacon and toss.

3. Also add whip cream and mustard, toss well and keep in the fridge until you serve it.

Enjoy!

(3) Italian Marinated Cauliflower Salad

This is so colored and delicious!

Prep Time: 1 hour and 10 minutes

Total Cooking Time: 1 hour and 20 minutes

Serving Size: 8

List of Ingredients:

- 1 Tbsp. sugar
- 1 carrot, halved and sliced
- Salt and black pepper to the taste
- 2 cups cauliflower florets
- ½ tsp. celery seeds
- ½ tsp. basil, dried
- 1 fennel bulb, sliced
- 1 cup green beans, halved
- ½ tsp. oregano, dried
- 3 garlic cloves, minced
- 1 red bell pepper, chopped
- ½ cup green olives, pitted and sliced
- 1 yellow bell pepper, chopped
- 2 Tbsp. dill, chopped
- 3 Tbsp. parsley, chopped
- 2 red hot chilies, chopped
- 2 celery stalks, chopped
- ¾ cup cider vinegar
- ½ cup red onion, chopped
- 2 Tbsp. olive oil
- ½ cup water
- ¾ cup white vinegar

Instructions:

1. Put green beans, cauliflower and carrot in a pot, add water to cover, bring to a boil over medium high heat.

2. Cook mixture for 3 minutes, transfer them to a bowl filled with ice water, drain, transfer to a bowl and mix with fennel, yellow and red bell pepper, celery, red onion, hot chilies and green olives and toss.

3. In a pot, mix the water with vinegar, garlic, cider vinegar, celery seeds, basil, oregano, salt, pepper and sugar, stir, bring to a boil over medium heat, boil for 10 minutes, add to cauliflower mix and leave aside for 1 hour.

4. Also add oil, parsley and dill, toss well and serve.

Enjoy!

(4) Creamy Cauliflower Salad

This is so tasty and creamy! We adore this salad!

Prep Time: 10 minutes

Total Cooking Time: 15 minutes

Serving Size: 6

List of Ingredients:

- 1 cauliflower head, florets separated
- 2 celery ribs, chopped
- 1 cup red onion, chopped
- ½ cup sour cream
- 1 Tbsp. lemon juice
- 1 tsp. grainy brown mustard
- 2 Tbsp. Dijon mustard
- ½ tsp. sugar
- Salt and black pepper to the taste

MMMMMMMMMMMMMMMMMMMMMMMMMMMMMMMMMMM

Instructions:

1. Put cauliflower in a pot, add water to cover, bring to a simmer, cook for 5 minutes, drain, put in a bowl, add celery and red onion and toss.

2. In a separate bowl, mix sour cream with brown mustard, Dijon mustard, lemon juice, sugar, salt and pepper and whisk really well.

3. Add this to cauliflower mix, toss and serve.

Enjoy!

(5) Cauliflower Antipasto Salad

This is just so delicious!

Prep Time: 10 minutes

Total Cooking Time: 10 minutes

Serving Size: 6

List of Ingredients:

- ½ cup green olives, pitted and sliced
- 3 cups cauliflower florets
- ½ cup black olives, pitted and sliced
- ¼ cup banana pepper ring
- ½ cup red bell pepper, chopped
- 2 Tbsp. pine nuts
- 1 Tbsp. lemon juice
- 2 Tbsp. cider vinegar
- Salt and black pepper to the taste
- ¼ cup olive oil
- 1 tsp. Italian herbs, dried

MMMMMMMMMMMMMMMMMMMMMMMMMMMMMMMMMM

Instructions:

1. In a salad bowl, mix cauliflower with green olives, black olives, banana pepper, red bell pepper, pine nuts, salt and pepper and toss.

2. In a separate bowl, mix lemon juice with vinegar, oil, salt, pepper and Italian herbs and whisk well.

3. Add this over your cauliflower salad, toss and serve.

Enjoy!

(6) Cauliflower and Artichokes
Salad

This is really good and so delicious!

Prep Time: 10 minutes

Total Cooking Time: 20 minutes

Serving Size: 4

List of Ingredients:

- 1 cauliflower head, florets separated
- 1-pound brown mushrooms, halved
- 16 ounces canned and marinated artichoke hearts
- ½ cup olive oil
- 1 cup cider vinegar
- 1 garlic clove, minced
- Salt and black pepper to the taste
- ½ tsp. peppercorns
- ½ tsp. thyme, dried
- ½ tsp. oregano, dried

MMMMMMMMMMMMMMMMMMMMMMMMMMMMMMM

Instructions:

1. Heat up a pan with half of the oil over medium high heat, add mushrooms, stir, sauté for 5 minutes and transfer to a large bowl.

2. Put cauliflower florets in a pot, add water to cover, bring to a boil over medium heat, cook for 4 minutes, drain and add to mushrooms.

3. Also add artichoke hearts, salt, pepper, peppercorns, thyme, oregano, garlic, vinegar and the rest of the oil, toss well and leave aside for a few hours before serving.

Enjoy!

(7) Cauliflower and Orange Salad

This is a raw salad everyone will love for sure!

Prep Time: 10 minutes

Total Cooking Time: 3 hours and 10 minutes

Serving Size: 2

List of Ingredients:

- ½ red bell pepper, chopped
- 2 cups cauliflower, chopped
- 1 ½ cups mandarin orange segments
- ½ cup broccoli, chopped
- 3 Tbsp. olive oil
- 3 Tbsp. lemon juice
- ½ tsp. lemon zest, grated
- 1 tsp. honey
- Salt and black pepper to the taste

MMMMMMMMMMMMMMMMMMMMMMMMMMMMMMMM

Instructions:

1. In a bowl, mix cauliflower with bell pepper, orange segments and broccoli.

2. Add oil, lemon juice, lemon zest, salt, pepper and honey, toss well and keep in the fridge for 3 hours before serving.

Enjoy!

(8) Cauliflower and Eggs Salad

This is so rich and textured!

Prep Time: 2 hours and 10 minutes

Total Cooking Time: 2 hours and 10 minutes

Serving Size: 6

List of Ingredients:

- 1 big cauliflower head, florets separated and roughly chopped
- 1 Tbsp. mustard
- ¾ cup mayonnaise
- 3 eggs, hard boiled, peeled and chopped
- Salt and black pepper to the taste
- ¼ cup dill pickle, chopped
- 1 yellow onion, chopped
- 3 bacon slices, cooked and crumbled

MMMMMMMMMMMMMMMMMMMMMMMMMMMMMMMMM

Instructions:

1. In a large salad bowl, mix cauliflower with pickle, onion and eggs and toss.

2. Add mustard, mayo, salt, pepper and bacon, toss well and keep in the fridge for 2 hours before serving.

Enjoy!

(9) Cauliflower and Carrots Salad

This veggie salad is so awesome and delicious!

Prep Time: 10 minutes

Total Cooking Time: 10 minutes

Serving Size: 8

List of Ingredients:

- 1 cauliflower head, florets separated
- 3 carrots, shredded
- 3 celery ribs, chopped
- ½ cup pimiento stuffed green olives
- ¼ cup olive oil
- ½ cup celery leaves, chopped
- ¼ cup water
- ¼ cup white vinegar
- 1 tsp. sugar
- Salt and black pepper to the taste

MMMMMMMMMMMMMMMMMMMMMMMMMMMMMMMMMMMM

Instructions:

1. In a salad bowl, mix cauliflower with carrots, celery ribs and green olives and toss.

2. In your blender, mix celery leaves with oil, water, sugar, vinegar, salt and pepper and blend well.

3. Add this over salad, toss and serve cold.

Enjoy!

(10) Fresh Cauliflower and Chestnut Salad

This is so refreshing and delicious!

Prep Time: 10 minutes

Total Cooking Time: 10 minutes

Serving Size: 6

List of Ingredients:

- 1 cauliflower head, florets separated
- 7 ounces canned water chestnuts, drained
- ¾ cup mayonnaise
- ½ cup yellow onion, chopped
- 1 cup radish, sliced
- ¾ cup sour cream

MMMMMMMMMMMMMMMMMMMMMMMMMMMMMMMMMM

Instructions:

1. In a salad bowl, mix cauliflower with water chestnuts, onion, radish, mayo and sour cream, toss well and serve right away.

Enjoy!

Chapter II - Special and Really Awesome Cauliflower Side Dishes

We recommend you to try each of our awesome cauliflower side dish recipes! We can assure you that you will adore them!

MMMMMMMMMMMMMMMMMMMMMMMMMMMMMMMMM

(11) Skillet Cauliflower Mix

This is a rich and flavored cauliflower side dish!

Prep Time: 10 minutes

Total Cooking Time: 20 minutes

Serving Size: 4

List of Ingredients:

- 1 ½ cups milk
- 4 cups cauliflower florets
- ½ tsp. olive oil
- 1 cup cheddar cheese, grated
- ½ cup bread crumbs
- Salt and black pepper to the taste
- 2 Tbsp. white flour
- 1 Tbsp. chives, chopped
- 1 tsp. mustard

MMMMMMMMMMMMMMMMMMMMMMMMMMMMMMMMM

Instructions:

1. Heat up a pot with the half of the milk over medium high heat, add cauliflower, stir and simmer for 5 minutes.

2. In a bowl, mix breadcrumbs with half of the cheese and oil and stir.

3. In a second bowl, mix flour with the rest of the milk and stir well.

4. Add this over cauliflower, also add the rest of the cheese, salt, pepper, chives and mustard and stir.

5. Add bread crumbs, stir, introduce in preheated broiler and broil for 3 minutes.

6. Divide on plates and serve as a side dish.

Enjoy!

(12) Delicious Cauliflower Casserole

This is so rich and delicious! It's one of our favorite side dishes!

Prep Time: 10 minutes

Total Cooking Time: 1 hour

Serving Size: 12

List of Ingredients:

- 4 garlic cloves, minced
- 4 Tbsp. butter
- Salt and black pepper to the taste
- 3 cups milk
- ⅓ cup white flour
- 2 cauliflower heads, florets separated
- 1 and ⅓ cup parmesan, grated
- ¼ cup chives, chopped
- 3 Tbsp. sesame seeds, toasted
- 1 ½ tsp. caraway seeds
- 1 Tbsp. poppy seeds

MMMMMMMMMMMMMMMMMMMMMMMMMMMMMMMM

Instructions:

1. Heat up a pan with the butter over medium high heat, add garlic, salt and pepper, stir and cook for 1-2 minutes.

2. Add flour, stir well and cook for 1-2 minutes more.

3. Add milk, whisk well and cook for 1-2 minutes.

4. Add chives and cauliflower stir and pour everything in a baking pan.

5. Introduce in the oven and bake at 425°F for 40 minutes.

6. Meanwhile, in a bowl, mix cheese with sesame seeds, caraway seeds, salt, pepper and poppy seeds, stir, sprinkle over cauliflower casserole, introduce in the oven and bake for 2 minutes more.

7. Divide on plates and serve as a side dish.

Enjoy!

(13) Delightful Cauliflower Gratin

This is so rich and flavored! You really have to make this at home!

Prep Time: 10 minutes

Total Cooking Time: 45 minutes

Serving Size: 12

List of Ingredients:

- 2 cups milk
- 14 cups cauliflower and broccoli florets
- ½ tsp. garlic powder
- Salt and black pepper to the taste
- 1 and ½ tsp. mustard
- 1 cup cheddar cheese, grated
- ¾ cup gruyere cheese, grated
- ¼ cup chives, chopped
- 1 cup crackers, crushed
- 2 tsp. olive oil
- 2 Tbsp. cornstarch mixed with 2 Tbsp. water

MMMMMMMMMMMMMMMMMMMMMMMMMMMMMMMMMM

Instructions:

1. Put some water in a pot, add cauliflower and broccoli florets, bring to a boil, cook for 1 minute, drain well and spread on a plate.

2. In a separate pot, combine milk with salt, pepper, garlic powder and mustard, stir and bring to a boil over medium heat.

3. Add cornstarch mix, stir really well and bring to a simmer.

4. Add cheddar, chives and gruyere, stir well and take off heat.

5. Add broccoli and cauliflower florets, toss and spread in a greased baking dish.

6. In a separate bowl, mix crackers with oil, toss and sprinkle over cauliflower gratin.

7. Introduce in the oven at 375°F and bake for 30 minutes.

8. Cool gratin down, slice and serve as a side dish.

Enjoy!

(14) Classic Cauliflower Side Dish

This is so satisfying and delicious!

Prep Time: 10 minutes

Total Cooking Time: 20 minutes

Serving Size: 4

List of Ingredients:

- ½ cup water
- 2 Tbsp. hoisin sauce
- 1 Tbsp. dry sherry
- 1 Tbsp. soy sauce
- 1 Tbsp. rice vinegar
- 1 Tbsp. cornstarch
- 4 cups cauliflower florets
- 2 scallions, chopped
- 3 Tbsp. olive oil
- 2 garlic cloves, minced
- 1 cup shelled edamame

MMMMMMMMMMMMMMMMMMMMMMMMMMMMMMMM

Instructions:

1. In a bowl, mix hoisin sauce with water, soy sauce, vinegar, cornstarch and sherry and whisk.

2. Heat up a pan with the oil over medium high heat, add cauliflower, stir and brown for 6 minutes.

3. Add scallions and garlic, stir and cook for 1 minute.

4. Add edamame, stir and cook for 3 minutes more.

5. Add hoisin sauce mix, stir, cook for 1 minute more, divide on plates and serve as a side dish.

Enjoy!

(15) Roasted Balsamic Cauliflower

This is so yummy and easy to make! It's a great side dish!

Prep Time: 10 minutes

Total Cooking Time: 40 minutes

Serving Size: 4

List of Ingredients:

- 8 cups cauliflower florets
- Salt and black pepper to the taste
- 2 Tbsp. olive oil
- 2 Tbsp. balsamic vinegar
- ½ cup parmesan, grated
- 1 tsp. marjoram, dried

MMMMMMMMMMMMMMMMMMMMMMMMMMMMMMM

Instructions:

1. In a bowl, mix cauliflower with salt, pepper, marjoram and oil, toss well and spread on a lined baking sheet.

2. place in the oven at 450°F and bake for 20 minutes.

3. Add vinegar and cheese, toss, bake for 10 minutes more, divide on plates and serve as a side dish.

Enjoy!

(16) Delicious Cauliflower and Sauce

This is an amazing combination!

Prep Time: 10 minutes

Total Cooking Time: 35 minutes

Serving Size: 8

List of Ingredients:

- Cooking spray
- 1 cup milk
- Salt and black pepper to the taste
- 3 cauliflower heads, florets separated
- ½ cup gruyere cheese, shredded
- 2 Tbsp. chives, chopped
- ½ cup fontina cheese, shredded
- 1 Tbsp. olive oil
- 1 Tbsp. white flour

MMMMMMMMMMMMMMMMMMMMMMMMMMMMMMMM

Instructions:

1. Spray a baking sheet with cooking spray, add cauliflower florets, season with salt and pepper and spread well.

2. Introduce them in the oven and bake at 425°F for 20 minutes.

3. Meanwhile, heat up a pan with the olive oil over medium heat, add flour and milk and whisk really well.

4. Add fontina cheese, gruyere cheese and chives, stir, cook for 1 minute and take off heat.

5. Divide cauliflower on plates, spread cheese sauce all over and serve as a side dish.

Enjoy!

(17) Braised Cauliflower

This is delicious and healthy at the same time!

Prep Time: 10 minutes

Total Cooking Time: 27 minutes

Serving Size: 6

List of Ingredients:

- 3 Tbsp. olive oil
- ½ tsp. coriander, ground
- ¼ tsp. allspice, ground
- Salt and black pepper to the taste
- 6 cups cauliflower florets
- 4 cups tomatoes, chopped
- 2 garlic cloves, minced
- ½ cup shallots, chopped
- 1 Tbsp. marjoram, chopped
- ½ tsp. cumin, ground

MMMMMMMMMMMMMMMMMMMMMMMMMMMMMMM

Instructions:

1. Heat up a pan with 2 Tbsp. oil over medium high heat, add garlic and shallots, stir and cook for 1 minute.

2. Add cumin, marjoram, coriander, salt, pepper and allspice, stir and cook for a few seconds more.

3. Add cauliflower, tomatoes and the rest of the oil, toss, cover and cook for 10 minutes.

4. Uncover pan, cook cauliflower mix for 4 minutes more, divide on plates and serve as a side dish.

Enjoy!

(18) Cauliflower with Cilantro

This is so fresh and tasty! It's a great side dish!

Prep Time: 10 minutes

Total Cooking Time: 40 minutes

Serving Size: 4

List of Ingredients:

- 1 cauliflower head, florets separated
- Salt and black pepper to the taste
- Juice from ½ lime
- ½ red chili, chopped
- 1 Tbsp. coconut oil
- 1 Tbsp. cilantro, chopped
- 2 Tbsp. coriander, ground

MMMMMMMMMMMMMMMMMMMMMMMMMMMMMMMMMM

Instructions:

1. Arrange cauliflower florets in a baking sheet, add oil, salt and pepper and toss.

2. Add coriander, lime juice and chili pepper, toss, introduce in the oven at 400°F and bake for 30 minutes.

3. Sprinkle cilantro on top, toss again, divide on plates and serve as a side dish.

Enjoy!

(19) Special Mashed Cauliflower

Forget about mashed potatoes! Try this special side dish for a change!

Prep Time: 10 minutes

Total Cooking Time: 23 minutes

Serving Size: 6

List of Ingredients:

- 3 Tbsp. olive oil
- Salt and black pepper to the taste
- 8 cups cauliflower florets
- 1 Tbsp. sage, chopped
- 2 garlic cloves, minced

MMMMMMMMMMMMMMMMMMMMMMMMMMMMMMMMMM

Instructions:

1. Put cauliflower in a pot, add water to cover, bring to a boil over medium high heat, cook for 10 minutes, drain and put in your food processor.

2. Heat up a pan with half of the oil over medium heat, add garlic, stir and cook for 1 minute.

3. Add this over cauliflower, also add salt, pepper and sage, pulse well, add the rest of the oil, pulse again, divide on plates and serve as a side dish.

Enjoy!

(20) Cauliflower Pilaf

This tastes a lot better than rice pilaf! Try it!

Prep Time: 10 minutes

Total Cooking Time: 15 minutes

Serving Size: 4

List of Ingredients:

- 1 cauliflower head, florets separated
- ¼ cup almonds, chopped
- 2 tsp. lemon zest
- 3 Tbsp. olive oil
- ¼ cup parsley, chopped
- Salt and black pepper to the taste
- 2 garlic cloves, minced

MMMMMMMMMMMMMMMMMMMMMMMMMMMMMMMMMM

Instructions:

1. Put cauliflower in your food processor and pulse until you obtain a cauliflower "rice".

2. Heat up a pan with the oil over medium heat, add garlic, stir and cook for 1 minute.

3. Add cauliflower rice, salt, pepper, lemon zest, almonds and parsley, toss, cook for 4 minutes, divide on plates and serve as a side dish.

Enjoy!

Chapter III - The Best Cauliflower Appetizer and Snacks

You are about to discover some exciting cauliflower snacks and appetizer. Make them and we can assure you that everyone will appreciate you even more!

MMMMMMMMMMMMMMMMMMMMMMMMMMMMMMMMMM

(21) Simple Cauliflower Dip

Your friends will love this party dip! It's so creamy and rich!

Prep Time: 10 minutes

Total Cooking Time: 25 minutes

Serving Size: 12

List of Ingredients:

- 6 cups cauliflower florets
- Salt and black pepper to the taste
- 2 Tbsp. butter
- 8 garlic cloves, minced
- 4 cups veggie stock
- ½ cup milk
- A handful cilantro, chopped

MMMMMMMMMMMMMMMMMMMMMMMMMMMMMMMMMMMM

Instructions:

1. Heat up a pan with the butter over medium high heat, add garlic, stir, reduce temperature to low and cook for 5 minutes.

2. Meanwhile, put cauliflower in a pot, add stock, bring to a boil over medium heat, cook for 10 minutes and take off heat.

3. Transfer cauliflower to your blender, add 1 cup stock from the pot, also add salt, pepper, milk and sautéed garlic and pulse really well.

4. Divide this into bowls and serve as a delicious party dip.

Enjoy!

(22) Tasty Cauliflower Tots

This is the best snack ever!

Prep Time: 10 minutes

Total Cooking Time: 35 minutes

Serving Size: 40 pieces

List of Ingredients:

- 1 egg, whisked
- ½ cup onion, chopped
- 2 cups cauliflower florets
- ¼ cup bell pepper, chopped
- ¼ cup bread crumbs
- ½ cup cheddar cheese, shredded
- ¼ cup parmesan, grated
- ¼ cup cilantro, chopped
- Cooking spray
- Salt and black pepper to the taste

MMMMMMMMMMMMMMMMMMMMMMMMMMMMMMMMM

Instructions:

1. Put cauliflower in a pot, add some water to cover, boil over medium heat for 5 minutes, drain well, transfer to a blender and pulse well.

2. Transfer cauliflower to a bowl, add the egg, onion, bread crumbs, bell pepper, cheddar cheese, parmesan, salt, pepper and cilantro and stir well.

3. Shape ovals out of this mix, grease a lined baking sheet with cooking spray, arrange cauliflower tots, introduce in the oven at 375°F for 20 minutes.

4. Serve them with a dip.

Enjoy!

(23) Cauliflower Tortillas

You will adore these tortillas!

Prep Time: 10 minutes

Total Cooking Time: 32 minutes

Serving Size: 4

List of Ingredients:

- ¼ cup cilantro, chopped
- 1 cauliflower head, florets separated
- Juice from ½ lime
- Salt and black pepper to the taste

Instructions:

1. In your food processor, mix cauliflower with salt and pepper and pulse until you obtain a cauliflower rice.

2. Transfer riced cauliflower to a bowl, introduce in your microwave for 2 minutes, stir and cook in there for 2 minutes more.

3. Drain excess water using a kitchen towel and transfer cauliflower to another bowl.

4. Add lime juice, salt, pepper and cilantro, stir well and shape 4 tortillas out of this mix.

5. Arrange them all on a lined baking sheet, bake in the oven at 375°F for 10 minutes, flip and bake for 7 minutes more.

6. Heat up a pan over medium high heat, add 1 cauliflower tortilla, brown for 2 minutes on each side and transfer to a bowl.

7. Repeat with the rest of the tortillas and serve them as a snack with a tasty dip.

Enjoy!

(24) Special Cauliflower "Wings"

This is a special snack!

Prep Time: 10 minutes

Total Cooking Time: 30 minutes

Serving Size: 6

List of Ingredients:

- 1 cauliflower head, florets separated
- ½ cup milk
- ½ cup flour
- ½ tsp. garlic powder
- Scallions, for serving

For the sauce:

- 2 Tbsp. lime juice
- ¼ cup honey
- 1 Tbsp. soy sauce
- ¼ cup sriracha sauce

MMMMMMMMMMMMMMMMMMMMMMMMMMMMMMMM

Instructions:

1. In a bowl, mix lime juice with honey, soy sauce and sriracha sauce, whisk well and leave aside for now.

2. In a separate bowl, mix cauliflower florets with flour milk and garlic powder and toss well.

3. Spread cauliflower "wings" on a lined baking sheet, introduce in the oven at 450°F and bake for 20 minutes.

4. Arrange cauliflower "wings" on a platter, sprinkle scallions on top and serve them with the sriracha sauce on the side.

Enjoy!

(25) Cauliflower Florets with Special Dressing

This is a really special cauliflower appetizer!

Prep Time: 10 minutes

Total Cooking Time: 40 minutes

Serving Size: 4

List of Ingredients:

- 1 cauliflower head, florets separated
- A pinch of salt and black pepper
- 2 Tbsp. sunflower seeds
- 1 avocado, pitted and peeled
- Juice from 1 lime
- 1 handful cilantro, chopped+ 1 Tbsp. cilantro, chopped
- 2 Tbsp. olive oil+ a drizzle of olive oil
- 1 garlic clove, minced
- 4 Tbsp. water

MMMMMMMMMMMMMMMMMMMMMMMMMMMMMMMMMM

Instructions:

1. Spread cauliflower florets on a lined baking sheet, drizzle some olive oil, season with a pinch of salt and pepper, toss them well, introduce in the oven at 425°F and roast them for 30 minutes, flipping them halfway.

2. Meanwhile, in your blender, mix avocado with lime juice, garlic, a handful cilantro, 2 Tbsp. olive oil, water, salt and pepper and pulse well.

3. Arrange cauliflower florets on a platter, drizzle avocado dressing all over, sprinkle 1 Tbsp. cilantro and sunflower seeds all over and serve as an appetizer.

Enjoy!

(26) Mini Cauliflower Pizza

This will really amaze everyone! It's the best appetizer!

Prep Time: 10 minutes

Total Cooking Time: 30 minutes

Serving Size: 8

List of Ingredients:

- ½ cup mozzarella, shredded
- ⅓ cup marinara sauce
- 2 Tbsp. basil, chopped
- ¼ cup mini pepperoni slices

For the mini pizzas crust:

- 1 egg
- 1 cauliflower head, chopped
- ⅓ cup mozzarella, shredded
- 2 Tbsp. parmesan, grated
- ½ tsp. garlic powder
- ½ tsp. oregano, dried
- 1 tsp. basil, dried
- ¼ tsp. onion powder
- Salt and black pepper to the taste

MMMMMMMMMMMMMMMMMMMMMMMMMMMMMMMMM

Instructions:

1. In your food processor, mix cauliflower with salt and pepper, pulse well, transfer to a bowl, cover and heat it your microwave for 5 minutes.

2. Drain cauliflower using a dish towel and transfer to another bowl.

3. Add egg, parmesan, ⅓ cup mozzarella, basil, oregano, garlic powder, salt, pepper and onion powder and stir well.

4. Shape medium circles out of this mix and arrange them all on a lined baking sheet.

5. Top each cauliflower pizza with pepperoni slices, marinara sauce and ½ cup mozzarella, introduce in the oven and bake at 425°F for 4 minutes.

6. Sprinkle basil on top, arrange pizzas on a platter and serve them.

Enjoy!

(27) Crazy Cauliflower Tacos

These are just so delicious!

Prep Time: 10 minutes

Total Cooking Time: 40 minutes

Serving Size: 12

List of Ingredients:

- 1 cauliflower head, florets separated
- 2 Tbsp. cilantro, chopped
- 1 cup rolled oats
- 2 tsp. chili powder
- 1 tsp. smoked paprika
- ¼ tsp. turmeric powder
- ½ tsp. cumin, ground
- A pinch of salt and pepper
- A pinch of cayenne pepper
- ¼ tsp. garlic powder
- 1 Tbsp. lime juice
- ¾ cup brown rice flour
- 1 and ¼ cups almond milk

For the slaw:

- ½ Tbsp. agave nectar
- 1 Tbsp. apple cider vinegar
- ¼ cup lime juice
- 2 cups purple cabbage, shredded
- A pinch of salt

For the avocado cream:

- 2 Tbsp. lime juice
- ¼ cup cilantro, chopped
- 1 avocado, pitted and peeled
- A pinch of salt

For serving:

- 12 corn tortillas, heated

MMMMMMMMMMMMMMMMMMMMMMMMMMMMMMM

Instructions:

1. Put rolled oats in your food processor, pulse them well and transfer to a bowl.

2. Add 2 Tbsp. cilantro, chili powder, smoked paprika, cumin, garlic powder, turmeric, salt, pepper and cayenne and toss well.

3. In a separate bowls, mix almond milk with 1 Tbsp. lime juice and rice flour and stir well.

4. Dip each cauliflower floret in almond milk batter, then in rolled oats mix, arrange them on a lined baking sheet and bake in the oven at 400°F for 30 minutes.

5. Meanwhile, purple cabbage with ¼ cup lime juice, apple cider vinegar, salt and agave nectar and toss well.

6. In your food processor, mix avocado with ¼ cup cilantro, 2 Tbsp. lime juice and some salt and blend well.

7. Divide cauliflower florets into taco shells, also divide cabbage slaw and top with avocado cream.

8. Arrange all tacos on a platter and serve.

Enjoy!

(28) Delicious Cauliflower Burgers

This tastes even better than a meat burger!

Prep Time: 10 minutes

Total Cooking Time: 20 minutes

Serving Size: 2

List of Ingredients:

- 1 cauliflower head
- ¼ cup parmesan, grated
- 1 cup panko bread crumbs
- Salt and black pepper to the taste
- ½ cup flour
- Vegetable oil for frying the burgers
- 2 eggs, whisked
- 2 buns, toasted and halved
- 2 provolone cheese slices
- Mayonnaise, for serving
- 2 lettuce leaves
- Roasted red pepper, sliced for serving

MMMMMMMMMMMMMMMMMMMMMMMMMMMMMMMMM

Instructions:

1. Cut cauliflower head on either side of the stem off, reserve these for another time and cut the rest of the head with the stem intact in half, creating 2 cauliflower "steaks".

2. Put cauliflower "steaks" in a pot, add water to cover, blanch them over medium heat for 3 minutes, drain on paper towels and leave them on a plate.

3. Meanwhile, in a bowl, mix panko bread crumbs with parmesan, salt and pepper and stir.

4. Put the eggs in a separate bowl.

5. Dip cauliflower "steaks" in parmesan and panko mix, then in egg mix and arrange them on a cutting board.

6. Heat up a pan with the oil over medium high heat, add "steaks", cook them for 2 minutes on each side and transfer them to paper towels to drain excess grease.

7. Divide steaks on 2 bun halves, top each with provolone cheese, spread mayo, add lettuce leaves, top with roasted peppers, cover with the other bun halves and serve.

Enjoy!

(29) Delicious Cauliflower Wraps

Try this appetizer really soon! It's incredibly delicious!

Prep Time: 10 minutes

Total Cooking Time: 25 minutes

Serving Size: 2

List of Ingredients:

- 1 Tbsp. sriracha sauce
- 8 romaine lettuce leaves
- 1 cauliflower head, florets separated
- 1 red bell pepper, sliced
- 1 red onion, chopped

For the sauce:

- 1 tsp. toasted sesame oil
- 2 Tbsp. sriracha sauce
- 2 Tbsp. peanut butter
- 2 Tbsp. almond milk
- 1 tsp. maple syrup
- ½ tsp. apple cider vinegar
- ½ tsp. turmeric powder

For the toppings:

- A handful cilantro, chopped
- Hemp seeds
- ¼ cup peanuts

MMMMMMMMMMMMMMMMMMMMMMMMMMMMMMMMM

Instructions:

1. Arrange cauliflower florets on a lined baking sheet, drizzle 1 Tbsp. sriracha sauce all over, introduce in the oven at 400°F and bake them for 10 minutes.

2. Add bell pepper slices and red onion and bake everything for 4 minutes more.

3. Meanwhile, in a bowl, mix 2 Tbsp. sriracha sauce with peanut butter, almond milk, sesame oil, vinegar, maple syrup and turmeric and whisk really well.

4. Arrange lettuce leaves on a platter, divide cauliflower and veggies mix on each, drizzle peanut butter sauce all over, top with peanuts, cilantro and hemp seeds and serve as an appetizer.

Enjoy!

(30) Easy Cauliflower Bites

This is a great snack for a movie night!

Prep Time: 10 minutes

Total Cooking Time: 40 minutes

Serving Size: 4

List of Ingredients:

- 1 cauliflower head, florets separated
- ½ cup water
- ½ cup white flour
- A splash of hot sauce
- ¼ tsp. dried onion
- A pinch of salt and black pepper
- ¼ cup buffalo sauce
- 3 Tbsp. melted butter
- Cooking spray

MMMMMMMMMMMMMMMMMMMMMMMMMMMMMMMMM

Instructions:

1. In a bowl, mix flour with water, hot sauce, salt, pepper and dried onion and whisk well.

2. Dip each cauliflower floret in this mix, arrange them all on a baking sheet which you've previously greased with cooking spray, place in the oven at 450°F and bake for 15 minutes.

3. Meanwhile, in a bowl, mix buffalo sauce with melted butter, a pinch of salt and pepper and whisk well.

4. Take cauliflower bites out of the oven, dip each in buffalo mix, arrange them again on your baking sheet and bake them for 8 minutes more.

5. Divide into bowls and serve as a snack.

Enjoy!

Chapter IV - Rich and Textured Cauliflower Soups and Stews

Who won't appreciate a delicious soup or a rich stew? We recommend you to try the best cauliflower soups and stews!

MMMMMMMMMMMMMMMMMMMMMMMMMMMMMMMMMM

(31) Sicilian Cauliflower Stew

How can you not adore this amazing stew?

Prep Time: 10 minutes

Total Cooking Time: 45 minutes

Serving Size: 2

List of Ingredients:

- 1 cauliflower head, florets separated
- 1 yellow onion, chopped
- 1 Tbsp. olive oil
- ½ tsp. chili flakes
- 1 garlic clove, minced
- ½ bunch parsley, chopped
- 2 Tbsp. black olives, pitted and sliced
- ¼ tsp. cinnamon, ground
- Salt and black pepper to the taste
- 1 Tbsp. raisins
- 12 ounces canned tomatoes, chopped
- 12 ounces canned chickpeas, drained

MMMMMMMMMMMMMMMMMMMMMMMMMMMMMMMM

Instructions:

1. Heat up a pot with the oil over medium heat, add onion, garlic and chili flakes, stir and cook for 3-4 minutes.

2. Add cauliflower, cinnamon, tomatoes and raisins, stir, cover pot and simmer stew for 15 minutes.

3. Add chickpeas, olives, salt and pepper, stir and cook for 15 minutes more.

4. Add parsley, stir, cook for 1-2 minutes, divide into bowls and serve.

Enjoy!

(32) Tasty and Light Cauliflower Soup

Try this light soup right away! Make it in your instant pot!

Prep Time: 10 minutes

Total Cooking Time: 20 minutes

Serving Size: 4

List of Ingredients:

- 2 Tbsp. butter
- 1 yellow onion, chopped
- 1 cauliflower head, florets separated and roughly chopped
- 3 cups chicken stock
- Salt and black pepper to the taste
- 1 tsp. garlic powder
- 4 ounces cream cheese, cubed
- 1 cup cheddar cheese, grated
- ½ cup half and half

MMMMMMMMMMMMMMMMMMMMMMMMMMMMMMMM

Instructions:

1. Set your instant pot on sauté mode, add butter, heat it up, add onion, stir and cook for 3 minutes.

2. Add cauliflower, stock, salt, pepper and garlic powder, stir, cover and cook on high for 5 minutes.

3. Blend soup using an immersion blender, add cream cheese, cheddar and half and half, stir, set the pot on sauté mode, cook soup for a few minutes more, ladle into bowls and serve.

Enjoy!

(33) Greek Cauliflower Stew

This is a really colorful and well flavored!

Prep Time: 10 minutes

Total Cooking Time: 30 minutes

Serving Size: 4

List of Ingredients:

- 1 cinnamon stick
- 1 Tbsp. olive oil
- 3 garlic cloves, minced
- 1 shallot, chopped
- 1 cauliflower head, florets separated
- Zest from ½ orange, grated
- 15 ounces tomato sauce
- 28 ounces canned tomatoes, crushed
- A pinch of red pepper flakes, crushed
- ½ tsp. celery seed
- 1 cup kalamata olives, pitted
- Salt and black pepper to the taste
- 1 tsp. oregano, dried

MMMMMMMMMMMMMMMMMMMMMMMMMMMMMMM

Instructions:

1. Heat up a pot with the oil over medium heat, add shallot and garlic, stir and cook for a few minutes.

2. Add cauliflower florets, cinnamon, orange zest, tomato sauce, tomatoes, oregano, pepper flakes and celery seed, stir, cover pot and cook stew for 15 minutes.

3. Add olives, salt and pepper, stir, divide into bowls and serve.

Enjoy!

(34) Roasted Cauliflower Soup

The taste is unbelievable! Try this soup as soon as possible!

Prep Time: 10 minutes

Total Cooking Time: 55 minutes

Serving Size: 6

List of Ingredients:

- 6 cups cauliflower florets
- 3 garlic cloves, minced
- 1 tsp. cumin, ground
- 2 Tbsp. olive oil+ 1 tsp.
- 1 tsp. turmeric powder
- A pinch of red pepper flakes, crushed
- Black pepper and salt to the taste
- 1 yellow onion, chopped
- 3 cups veggie stock
- 2 Tbsp. cilantro, chopped
- ¼ cup coconut milk

MMMMMMMMMMMMMMMMMMMMMMMMMMMMMMMMM

Instructions:

1. Arrange cauliflower and garlic on a lined baking sheet, season with salt, pepper, cumin, pepper flakes, turmeric and 2 Tbsp. oil, toss and roast in the oven at 450°F for 30 minutes.

2. Heat up a pot with 1 tsp. oil over medium heat, add onion, stir and cook for 3 minutes.

3. Add stock and roasted cauliflower, stir, cover pot and cook for 15 minutes.

4. Blend using an immersion blender, add coconut milk and cilantro, blend again, ladle into bowls and serve.

Enjoy!

(35) Indian Cauliflower Stew

This is really flavored and tasty!

Prep Time: 10 minutes

Total Cooking Time: 35 minutes

Serving Size: 6

List of Ingredients:

- 1 eggplant, cut in medium chunks
- 3 cups cauliflower florets
- 15 ounces canned tomatoes, chopped
- 1 tsp. garam masala
- 1 tsp. mustard seeds
- 2 Tbsp. curry powder
- 2 Tbsp. canola oil
- 1 yellow onion, chopped
- 2 garlic cloves, minced
- Salt and black pepper to the taste
- 1 tsp. ginger, grated
- 15 ounces canned chickpeas, chopped
- ½ cup water

MMMMMMMMMMMMMMMMMMMMMMMMMMMMMMMM

Instructions:

1. Heat up a pot over medium heat, add garam masala, curry powder and mustard seeds, stir, toast for 1 minute and transfer to a bowl.

2. Add oil to the pot, heat it up, add onion, ginger, garlic, salt and pepper, stir and cook for 3 minutes.

3. Add eggplant, cauliflower, chickpeas, tomatoes, water and garam masala mix, stir, bring to a simmer, cover and cook for 20 minutes.

4. Divide into bowls and serve hot.

Enjoy!

(36) Cauliflower and Red Pepper Soup

This soup is definitely in our top 5! Try it today!

Prep Time: 10 minutes

Total Cooking Time: 1 hour and 10 minutes

Serving Size: 4

List of Ingredients:

- 1 cauliflower head, florets separated
- 4 red bell peppers, halved
- 1 yellow onion, chopped
- 2 Tbsp. olive oil
- 2 garlic cloves, minced
- A pinch of red pepper flakes
- 1 tsp. thyme, chopped
- 4 cup chicken stock
- 4 ounces goat cheese, crumbled
- 1 tsp. smoked paprika
- Salt and black pepper to the taste

MMMMMMMMMMMMMMMMMMMMMMMMMMMMMMMM

Instructions:

1. Arrange red bell peppers on a lined baking sheet, introduce in preheated broiler and cook for 10 minutes.

2. Arrange cauliflower on another baking sheet, drizzle half of the oil over them, introduce in the oven at 400°F and roast for 20 minutes.

3. Heat up a pot with the rest of the oil over medium heat, add onion, stir and cook for 6 minutes.

4. Add pepper flakes, thyme and garlic, stir and cook for 1 minute.

5. Add peeled and chopped red bell peppers, stock, cauliflower, goat cheese and paprika, stir and cook for 10 minutes.

6. Blend using an immersion blender, season with salt and pepper, stir, ladle into bowls and serve.

Enjoy!

(37) Hearty Cauliflower Stew

This is truly a fulfilling stew!

Prep Time: 10 minutes

Total Cooking Time: 30 minutes

Serving Size: 4

List of Ingredients:

- 1 cauliflower head, florets separated
- 1 tsp. cumin seeds
- 2 Tbsp. coconut oil
- 1 yellow onion, chopped
- 3 tomatoes, chopped
- 1 cup kale, chopped
- 1 jalapeno, chopped
- 14 ounces coconut milk
- Salt and black pepper to the taste
- 2 tsp. ginger paste
- 1 Tbsp. coriander powder
- 1 Tbsp. cumin powder
- 1 tsp. turmeric powder
- 2 Tbsp. cilantro, chopped

MMMMMMMMMMMMMMMMMMMMMMMMMMMMMMMMM

Instructions:

1. Heat up a pot with the oil over medium heat, add cumin seeds, stir and cook for 30 seconds.

2. Add onion, stir and cook for 1 minute.

3. Add tomatoes, stir and cook for 2 minutes more.

4. Add cauliflower, kale, jalapeno, coconut milk, salt, pepper, ginger paste, coriander, cumin, turmeric and cilantro, stir, cover pot and cook over medium heat for 15 minutes.

5. Divide into bowls and serve.

Enjoy!

(38) Slow Cooked Cauliflower Soup

You will be really impressed with this soup!

Prep Time: 10 minutes

Total Cooking Time: 6 hours and 10 minutes

Serving Size: 4

List of Ingredients:

- 2 garlic cloves, minced
- 2 cups cauliflower florets
- 3 cups broccoli florets, chopped
- ½ cup shallots, chopped
- 1 carrot, chopped
- 3 and ½ cups veggie stock
- Salt and black pepper to the taste
- 1 cup milk
- 1 cup Greek yogurt
- 6 ounces cheddar cheese, shredded

MMMMMMMMMMMMMMMMMMMMMMMMMMMMMMMMMM

Instructions:

1. In your slow cooker, mix cauliflower with broccoli, garlic, shallots, carrots, salt, pepper and stock, stir, cover and cook on low for 5 hours and 30 minutes.

2. Add milk, stir, cover and cook on low for 30 minutes more.

3. Add cheese and yogurt, stir well, ladle into bowls and serve.

Enjoy!

(39) Flavored Cauliflower Stew

This cauliflower stew is absolutely amazing and delicious!

Prep Time: 10 minutes

Total Cooking Time: 1 hour

Serving Size: 6

List of Ingredients:

- 1 ½ tsp. cinnamon powder
- 1 ½ tsp. turmeric powder
- 1 ½ tsp. cumin, ground
- 1 tsp. coriander, ground
- 1 tsp. sweet paprika
- A pinch of cayenne pepper
- 5 carrots, roughly chopped
- 1 cauliflower head, florets separated
- 1 ½ tsp. green cardamom
- 2 Tbsp. olive oil + a drizzle
- 1 yellow onion, chopped
- 28 ounces canned tomatoes, chopped
- 6 garlic cloves, minced
- 28 ounces canned chickpeas, drained
- ½ cup parsley, chopped

MMMMMMMMMMMMMMMMMMMMMMMMMMMMMMMMMM

Instructions:

1. In a bowl, mix cinnamon with turmeric, cumin, coriander, paprika, cayenne, cardamom, cauliflower, carrots and oil, toss well, arrange on a lined baking sheet, introduce in the oven at 475°F and roast for 20 minutes.

2. Heat up a pot with 2 Tbsp. oil over medium heat, add onion, stir and cook for 2 minutes.

3. Add garlic, stir and cook for 2 minutes more.

4. Add tomatoes, chickpeas, cauliflower and carrots, salt and pepper, stir, bring to a boil and cook for 20 minutes.

5. Add parsley, stir, divide into bowls and serve.

Enjoy!

(40) Cauliflower and Sweet Potato Soup

This is so satisfying and delicious!

Prep Time: 10 minutes

Total Cooking Time: 50 minutes

Serving Size: 8

List of Ingredients:

- 2 pounds cauliflower florets, chopped
- 3 sweet potatoes, cubed
- 2 celery stalks, chopped
- 1 yellow onion, chopped
- 1 carrot, chopped
- 4 garlic cloves, minced
- 4 green onions, chopped
- 30 ounces chicken stock
- ½ tsp. thyme, dried
- 1 tsp. sweet paprika
- 2 cups milk
- Salt and black pepper to the taste
- ¼ cup flour
- Bacon, cooked and crumbled

MMMMMMMMMMMMMMMMMMMMMMMMMMMMMMMMMM

Instructions:

1. In a pot, mix cauliflower with sweet potatoes, celery, onion, carrot, garlic, green onions, stock, thyme, paprika, salt and pepper, stir, bring to a boil over medium heat, cover and cook for 30 minutes.

2. In a bowl, combine milk with flour, stir well, add to soup, cook soup for 5 minutes more, blend using an immersion blender, ladle into bowls and serve.

Enjoy!

Chapter V - The Most Delicious and Incredible Cauliflower Breakfasts

Did you know you could use cauliflower to make some amazing breakfast recipes? It's time you discover them all!

MMMMMMMMMMMMMMMMMMMMMMMMMMMMMMMMMM

(41) Breakfast Cauliflower and Broccoli Cakes

These are just awesome! Everyone will ask for more!

Prep Time: 10 minutes

Total Cooking Time: 40 minutes

Serving Size: 8

List of Ingredients:

- ½ cauliflower head, florets separated
- ½ broccoli head, florets separated
- 3 ounces cheddar cheese, grated
- A handful parsley, chopped
- 2 tsp. cumin, ground
- ¾ cup sunflower seeds
- 1 tsp. paprika
- Black pepper and salt to taste
- 3 eggs
- 3 Tbsp. psyllium husks

MMMMMMMMMMMMMMMMMMMMMMMMMMMMMMMMMM

Instructions:

1. In your food processor, mix cauliflower with broccoli, cheese, parsley, cumin, paprika, salt, pepper, eggs and psyllium husks and pulse well until you obtain a sticky dough.

2. Shape medium cakes out of this mix, arrange them on a lined baking sheet, put in the oven at 400°F for 30 minutes.

3. Serve them warm for breakfast.

Enjoy!

(42) Breakfast Cauliflower Muffins

You can even take these with you at the office!

Prep Time: 10 minutes

Total Cooking Time: 30 minutes

Serving Size: 4

List of Ingredients:

- 3 cups cauliflower, riced
- 6 ounces ham, chopped
- 5 eggs, whisked
- ½ cup baby spinach
- ½ cup yellow onion, chopped
- 1 cup cheddar cheese, shredded
- ½ tsp. garlic power
- A pinch of salt
- A pinch of cayenne pepper
- Cooking spray

MMMMMMMMMMMMMMMMMMMMMMMMMMMMMMMMM

Instructions:

1. In a bowl, mix cauliflower with cauliflower with ham, eggs, spinach, onion, salt, cayenne pepper, garlic powder and cheddar cheese and whisk well.

2. Grease a muffin pan with cooking spray, divide cauliflower mix, introduce tray in the oven and bake muffins at 375°F for 20 minutes.

3. Leave muffins to cool down a bit and serve them for breakfast.

Enjoy!

(43) Cauliflower and Spinach Breakfast Cookies

This is so fulfilling! Try it today!

Prep Time: 10 minutes

Total Cooking Time: 30 minutes

Serving Size: 4

List of Ingredients:

- 1 Tbsp. olive oil
- 1 cups spinach, roughly chopped
- 1 cauliflower head, florets separated and ground
- 1 red onion, chopped
- ½ cup nuts, ground
- 3 eggs, whisked
- 2 garlic cloves, minced
- 1 Tbsp. parsley, chopped
- Salt and black pepper to the taste

MMMMMMMMMMMMMMMMMMMMMMMMMMMMMMMM

Instructions:

1. Heat up a pan with the oil over medium heat, add cauliflower, stir and cook for 10 minutes.

2. In a bowl, mix eggs with sautéed cauliflower, spinach, onion, nuts, garlic, salt, pepper and parsley and stir well.

3. Shape cookies using a cookie cutter out of this mix, place them on a lined baking sheet and bake in the oven at 350°F for 20 minutes.

4. Serve cookies warm for breakfast.

Enjoy!

(44) Cauliflower Bake

This is rich and so healthy!

Prep Time: 10 minutes

Total Cooking Time: 50 minutes

Serving Size: 6

List of Ingredients:

- 10 eggs
- 1 cauliflower head, grated
- 1 cup milk
- 8 bacon slices, chopped
- 2 tsp. sweet paprika
- 2 garlic cloves, minced
- Salt and black pepper to the taste
- 2 green onions, chopped
- 2 cups cheddar cheese, shredded
- Hot sauce, for serving

MMMMMMMMMMMMMMMMMMMMMMMMMMMMMMMMMMM

Instructions:

1. Heat up a pan over medium high heat, add bacon, cook until it's crispy, transfer to paper towels, drain grease and leave aside.

2. In a bowl, mix eggs with garlic, milk, salt, pepper and paprika and whisk well.

3. Spread cauliflower in a baking dish, top with cooked bacon, cheddar cheese, green onions and eggs mix.

4. Put this in the oven, bake at 375°F for 40 minutes, cool down a bit, slice and serve for breakfast.

Enjoy!

(45) Cauliflower Omelet

This is so yummy and it's going to be ready in no time! Try it!

Prep Time: 10 minutes

Total Cooking Time: 30 minutes

Serving Size: 4

List of Ingredients:

- 2 ½ Tbsp. olive oil
- 5 eggs, whisked
- 1 garlic clove, minced
- 1 small cauliflower head, florets separated
- 2 ounces feta cheese, crumbled
- ¼ cup parsley, chopped

MMMMMMMMMMMMMMMMMMMMMMMMMMMMMMMMMMM

Instructions:

1. Heat up a pan with the oil over medium high heat, add cauliflower, stir and cook for 10 minutes.

2. Add garlic, salt and pepper and cook for 1 minute more.

3. Add eggs, spread them into the pan, cook for 5 minutes and flip.

4. Cook omelet for 2 minutes more, divide on plates, sprinkle feta and parsley on top and serve.

Enjoy!

(46) Breakfast Cauliflower Hash Browns

This is one of our favorite cauliflower breakfasts!

Prep Time: 10 minutes

Total Cooking Time: 25 minutes

Serving Size: 6

List of Ingredients:

- 3 cups cauliflower, grated
- 1 egg
- A pinch of cayenne pepper
- 1 cup cheddar cheese, grated
- Salt and black pepper to the taste

MMMMMMMMMMMMMMMMMMMMMMMMMMMMMMMMMMMM

Instructions:

1. In a bowl, mix cauliflower with egg, salt, pepper, cayenne and cheddar cheese, stir well, shape 6 square hash browns and arrange them all on a lined baking sheet.

2. Bake hash browns in the oven at 400°F for 15 minutes, cool them down and serve for breakfast.

Enjoy!

(47) Tasty Cauliflower and Beef Breakfast Hash

This is a really good combination! Try it soon!

Prep Time: 10 minutes

Total Cooking Time: 30 minutes

Serving Size: 4

List of Ingredients:

- 2 cups corned beef, chopped
- 2 cups cauliflower florets, chopped
- 1 Tbsp. olive oil
- Salt and black pepper to the taste
- ½ cup yellow onion, chopped

MMMMMMMMMMMMMMMMMMMMMMMMMMMMMMMMM

Instructions:

1. Heat up a pan with the oil over medium heat, add beef, stir and cook for 6 minutes.

2. Add cauliflower, stir a bit and cook for 8 minutes more.

3. Add onions, salt and pepper, stir and cook for 5 minutes.

4. Divide on plates and serve for breakfast.

Enjoy!

(48) Cauliflower Breakfast Bowls

This veggie mix will taste so good!

Prep Time: 10 minutes

Total Cooking Time: 22 minutes

Serving Size: 2

List of Ingredients:

- 1 avocado, pitted, peeled and roughly chopped
- A pinch of garlic powder
- Salt and black pepper to the taste
- Juice from ½ lime
- 2 eggs
- A drizzle of olive oil
- 1 and ½ cups cauliflower, grated
- 4 ounces mushrooms, sliced
- A handful baby spinach
- 1 green onion, chopped
- Salsa for serving

MMMMMMMMMMMMMMMMMMMMMMMMMMMMMMMM

Instructions:

1. In a bowl, mix avocado with lime juice, salt, pepper and garlic powder, mash well and leave aside for now.

2. Heat up a pan with a drizzle of oil over medium heat, add mushrooms, salt and pepper, stir, cook for 2-3 minutes and transfer to a bowl.

3. Heat up the same pan over medium high heat, add cauliflower, salt, pepper and garlic powder, stir, cook for 5 minutes and transfer to another bowl.

4. Heat up the pan again over medium high heat, return mushrooms to pan, add baby spinach and green onion, stir and cook for 1 minute.

5. Add whisked eggs, salt and pepper and cook until eggs are scrabbled.

6. Add this mix to cauliflower, toss, divide into 2 bowls, top with mashed avocado and salsa and serve.

Enjoy!

(49) Delicious Cauliflower Frittata

It's so healthy and easy to make! Make it for breakfast tomorrow!

Prep Time: 10 minutes

Total Cooking Time: 30 minutes

Serving Size: 4

List of Ingredients:

- 1 yellow onion, chopped
- 2 Tbsp. olive oil
- 1 tsp. thyme, chopped
- Salt and black pepper to the taste
- ½ tsp. smoked paprika
- 8 eggs
- ¼ cup water
- 2 cups cauliflower florets
- ½ cup goat cheese, crumbled
- 3 garlic cloves, minced
- 5 cups kale, chopped

MMMMMMMMMMMMMMMMMMMMMMMMMMMMMMMMM

Instructions:

1. Heat up a pan with 1 Tbsp. oil over medium heat, add onion, stir and cook for 4 minutes.

2. Add water and cauliflower, stir, cover pan and cook for 6 minutes.

3. Add garlic, thyme, salt, pepper and kale, stir and cook for 3 minutes more.

4. In a bowl, mix eggs with salt, pepper and paprika and stir.

5. Add veggies mix from the pan and toss gently.

6. Clean the pan, add the rest of the oil, heat up over medium high heat, add eggs mix, spread, top with cheese, cover pan and cook everything for 5 minutes.

7. Broil frittata for 3 minutes in heated broiler, slice, divide on plates and serve for breakfast.

Enjoy!

(50) Delicious Cauliflower Skillet

This is a light cauliflower breakfast full of amazing tastes!

Prep Time: 10 minutes

Total Cooking Time: 50 minutes

Serving Size: 6

List of Ingredients:

- 16 ounces cauliflower florets
- 12 ounces chicken sausage, ground
- 1 red onion, chopped
- ¼ tsp. Italian seasoning
- A pinch of salt and black pepper
- ½ cup milk
- 12 eggs
- 12 ounces cheddar cheese, shredded
- Green onions, chopped for serving

MMMMMMMMMMMMMMMMMMMMMMMMMMMMMMMMMM

Instructions:

1. Heat up a skillet over medium high heat, add chicken sausage, cauliflower and onion, stir and sauté for 3-4 minutes.

2. Add salt, pepper, Italian seasoning and half of the cheddar and stir.

3. In a bowl, mix milk with eggs, whisk well and pour over cauliflower mix.

4. Stir gently, sprinkle the rest of the cheddar cheese on top, introduce skillet in the oven at 350°F and bake for 35-40 minutes.

5. Sprinkle green onions on top and serve for breakfast.

Enjoy!

Chapter VI - Incredible Cauliflower Main Dishes

These will surprise you for sure! These cauliflower main dish recipes are awesome!

MMMMMMMMMMMMMMMMMMMMMMMMMMMMMMMMM

(51) Tasty Cauliflower, Artichokes and Leeks

We can assure you this is really easy to make!

Prep Time: 10 minutes

Total Cooking Time: 30 minutes

Serving Size: 4

List of Ingredients:

- 1 ½ cups leeks, chopped
- 1 ½ cups cauliflower florets
- 2 garlic cloves, minced
- 1 ½ cups artichoke hearts
- 2 Tbsp. bacon grease
- Black pepper to the taste

MMMMMMMMMMMMMMMMMMMMMMMMMMMMMMMMMM

Instructions:

1. Heat up a pan with the bacon grease over medium high heat, add garlic, leeks, cauliflower florets and artichoke hearts, stir and cook for 20 minutes.

2. Add black pepper, stir, divide on plates and serve.

Enjoy!

(52) Cauliflower and Chicken Mix

Your guests will be really impressed with this dish!

Prep Time: 10 minutes

Total Cooking Time: 38 minutes

Serving Size: 6

List of Ingredients:

- 3 bacon slices, chopped
- 3 carrots, chopped
- 3 pounds chicken thighs, boneless and skinless
- 24 ounces cauliflower florets
- 2 bay leaves
- ¼ cup red wine vinegar
- 8 ounces canned tomatoes, chopped
- 4 garlic cloves, minced
- Salt and black pepper to the taste
- 4 Tbsp. olive oil
- 1 Tbsp. garlic powder
- 1 Tbsp. Italian seasoning
- 1 tsp. turmeric powder
- 1 cup beef stock

MMMMMMMMMMMMMMMMMMMMMMMMMMMMMMMMM

Instructions:

1. Set your instant pot on sauté mode, add bacon, carrots, onion and garlic, stir and cook for 8 minutes.

2. Add chicken, oil, vinegar, turmeric, garlic powder, Italian seasoning and bay leaves, stir, cover and cook on high for 20 minutes.

3. Add cauliflower and stock, stir, cover, cook on low for 4 minutes more, divide on plates and serve.

Enjoy!

(53) Cauliflower and Turnips Mix

This is a unique and delicious dish!

Prep Time: 10 minutes

Total Cooking Time: 1 hour and 10 minutes

Serving Size: 4

List of Ingredients:

- 6 cups cauliflower florets
- 1 ½ pounds turnips, thinly sliced
- 1 egg
- 2 cups chicken stock
- ¼ cup avocado oil
- A pinch of sea salt
- Black pepper to the taste

MMMMMMMMMMMMMMMMMMMMMMMMMMMMMMMM

Instructions:

1. Put stock in a pot, bring to a simmer over medium high heat, add cauliflower, stir, cover and cook for 15 minutes.

2. Transfer this to your food processor and blend well.

3. Add oil and blend well again.

4. In a bowl, whisk egg with 1 Tbsp. from the cauliflower mix.

5. Add this to cauliflower and pulse again well.

6. Add a pinch of salt and pepper and stir again.

7. Arrange turnips slices into a baking dish, pour the cauliflower purée over them, introduce in the oven at 375°F and bake for 30 minutes.

8. Divide on plates and serve.

Enjoy!

(54) Cauliflower and Cashew Sauce

This is a really unique and amazing combination!

Prep Time: 10 minutes

Total Cooking Time: 25 minutes

Serving Size: 5

List of Ingredients:

- 4 cups cauliflower florets
- 1 Tbsp. olive oil
- 1 ½ cups carrot, chopped
- 2 cups water
- ½ cup cashews
- ½ cup nutritional yeast
- Salt and black pepper to the taste
- 10 ounces canned tomatoes and green chilies, chopped
- 1 tsp. smoked paprika
- ½ tsp. chili powder
- ¼ tsp. mustard powder
- ½ tsp. jalapeno powder
- ½ cup cilantro, chopped

MMMMMMMMMMMMMMMMMMMMMMMMMMMMMMMM

Instructions:

1. In your instant pot, mix carrots water and cashews, stir, cover and cook on high for 5 minutes.

2. Strain this into a food processor, add salt, pepper, tomatoes and chilies, paprika, chili powder, mustard powder, jalapeno powder, cilantro and yeast, pulse, divide into bowls and leave aside.

3. Arrange cauliflower on a lined baking sheet, season with salt and pepper, drizzle olive oil all over, introduce in the oven at 375°F and bake for 15 minutes.

4. Arrange cauliflower on plates, drizzle cashew sauce all over and serve.

Enjoy!

(55) Cauliflower and Green Beans Mix

It's an amazing mix for you to try today!

Prep Time: 10 minutes

Total Cooking Time: 10 minutes

Serving Size: 4

List of Ingredients:

- 1-pound green beans, chopped
- 1 tomato, chopped
- ½ cup pecans, chopped
- Salt and black pepper to the taste
- ½ cauliflower head, chopped

For the pesto:

- ¼ cup olive oil
- 2 cups basil leaves
- 1 garlic clove, minced
- 1 Tbsp. lemon juice

MMMMMMMMMMMMMMMMMMMMMMMMMMMMMMMMMMMM

Instructions:

1. In your blender, mix basil with oil, garlic and lemon juice, pulse really well and leave aside for now.

2. In a salad bowl, mix green beans with cauliflower, tomato, pecans, salt and pepper and stir.

3. Add pesto, toss to coat well and serve.

Enjoy!

(56) Cauliflower and Potatoes Mix

You should really try this combination soon!

Prep Time: 10 minutes

Total Cooking Time: 1 hour and 10 minutes

Serving Size: 4

List of Ingredients:

- 2 cups cauliflower florets
- 8 medium potatoes
- 2 cups white mushrooms, roughly chopped
- 6 tomatoes, cubed
- 1 yellow onion, chopped
- 1 small garlic clove, minced
- ¼ tsp. onion powder
- 3 Tbsp. basil, chopped
- 3 Tbsp. parsley, chopped

MMMMMMMMMMMMMMMMMMMMMMMMMMMMMMMMMM

Instructions:

1. Place potatoes in the oven at 350°F, bake for 45 minutes, leave them aside to cool down, peel, chop them roughly and arrange on a lined baking sheet.

2. Add tomatoes, cauliflower, mushrooms, garlic, onion and onion powder, toss, introduce in the oven at 350°F and bake for 15 minutes.

3. Sprinkle basil and parsley on top, divide on plates and serve for breakfast.

Enjoy!

(57) Delicious Cauliflower and Mustard Vinaigrette

The combination is pretty great!

Prep Time: 10 minutes

Total Cooking Time: 10 minutes

Serving Size: 4

List of Ingredients:

- 1 cup cucumber, sliced
- 1 cup tomatoes, chopped
- 1 cauliflower head, florets chopped
- ¼ cup spring onion, chopped

For the salad dressing:

- 1 date, chopped
- ½ cup water
- ½ cup cashews, soaked and drained
- 2 Tbsp. coconut aminos
- 1 tsp. mustard powder
- 2 Tbsp. dill, chopped
- 2 garlic cloves, minced
- Zest and juice from ½ lemon
- Salt and black pepper to the taste
- ½ cup walnuts, chopped

MMMMMMMMMMMMMMMMMMMMMMMMMMMMMMMMMM

Instructions:

1. In your blender, mix cashews with water, date, mustard powder and coconut aminos and blend well.

2. Add dill, lemon zest and juice, garlic, walnuts, salt and pepper, blend again well and leave aside for now.

3. In a salad bowl, mix cauliflower with cucumber, tomato and onion and stir.

4. Add salad dressing you've made earlier and serve.

Enjoy!

(58) Cauliflower Curry

It's a special dish!

Prep Time: 10 minutes

Cooking time: 1 hour and 10 minutes

Serving Size: 6

List of Ingredients:

- 2 red chilies, chopped
- ¼ tsp. coconut sugar
- ½ cup water
- ¼ cup white vinegar
- Salt and black pepper to the taste
- 1 cauliflower head, florets separated
- ¼ cup olive oil
- 2 Tbsp. curry powder
- 2 shallots, chopped
- ¾ cup vegetable oil
- 15 ounces canned chickpeas, drained
- 1 yellow onion, chopped
- 1 small ginger piece, grated
- 2 tsp. tomato paste
- 1 tsp. lemongrass, grated
- 1 garlic clove, minced
- 1 tsp. harissa paste
- 13 ounces canned coconut milk
- 1 Tbsp. cilantro, chopped

MMMMMMMMMMMMMMMMMMMMMMMMMMMMMMMMM

Instructions:

1. In a bowl, mix vinegar with chilies, sugar, salt, pepper and half of the water, stir well and leave aside for now.

2. In a baking dish, mix cauliflower with the olive oil, salt and pepper, toss to coat introduce in the oven at 450°F, bake for 35 minutes, transfer to paper towels, drain fat and leave aside for now.

3. Heat up a pan with ½ cup vegetable oil over medium high heat, add shallots, stir, cook for 10 minutes, transfer to a bowl and leave aside as well.

4. Heat up another pan with the rest of the vegetable oil over medium high heat, add onion, stir and cook for 5 minutes.

5. Add garlic, ginger, lemongrass, stir and cook for 1 more minute.

6. Add harissa paste and tomato paste, stir and cook for 2 more minutes.

7. Add coconut milk, stir again, bring to a boil and cook for about 5 minutes.

8. Add chickpeas and the rest of the water, stir and bring to a boil again.

9. Take off heat, add cilantro, divide into bowls and serve with roasted cauliflower on the side, fried shallots and chilies on top.

Enjoy!

(59) Cauliflower and Chicken Curry

Even your most pretentious guests will love this dish!

Prep Time: 10 minutes

Total Cooking Time: 40 minutes

Serving Size: 6

List of Ingredients:

- A small ginger piece, grated
- 1 yellow onion, chopped
- 3 garlic cloves, minced
- 1 Tbsp. olive oil
- 2 red bell peppers, chopped
- 14 ounces coconut milk
- 2 Tbsp. maple syrup
- 2 Tbsp. yellow curry powder
- 2 tsp. turmeric powder
- 2 Tbsp. flour
- Salt and black pepper to the taste
- 4 cups cauliflower, florets separated and chopped
- ⅓ cup cilantro, chopped
- 1 ½ pounds chicken breasts, skinless, boneless and cubed
- ⅓ cup green onions, chopped

MMMMMMMMMMMMMMMMMMMMMMMMMMMMMMMM

Instructions:

1. Heat up a pot with the oil over medium heat, add onion, garlic, bell peppers and ginger, stir and cook for 7 minutes.

2. Add maple syrup, curry powder, turmeric, flour, chicken, cauliflower, salt and pepper, stir, bring to a boil, cover and simmer for 20 minutes.

3. Add green onions and cilantro, stir, divide on plates and serve with brown rice on the side.

Enjoy!

(60) Unbelievable Cauliflower Bars

This is really impressive!

Prep Time: 10 minutes

Total Cooking Time: 55 minutes

Serving Size: 12

List of Ingredients:

- 1 big cauliflower head, florets separated
- ½ cup mozzarella cheese, shredded
- ¼ cup egg whites
- 1 tsp. Italian seasoning
- Salt and black pepper to the taste
- Marinara sauce for serving

Directions:

1. Put cauliflower florets in your food processor, pulse until you obtain your cauliflower "rice" and spread on a lined baking sheet.

2. Introduce in the oven at 375°F and roast for 20 minutes.

3. Transfer to a bowl, cover with a towel and leave aside for 10 minutes.

4. Transfer cauliflower rice to your kitchen towel, wrap and squeeze excess liquid from it.

5. Put cauliflower into a clean bowl, add salt, pepper, almost all the cheese, egg whites and Italian seasoning and stir really well.

6. Spread this into a rectangle pan and press really well.

7. Introduce in the oven at 375°F and bake for 18 minutes.

8. Sprinkle the rest of the cheese, introduce in the oven and bake for 5 minutes more.

9. Cut in 12 bars, arrange them on a platter and serve warm with the marinara sauce on the side.

Enjoy!

Chapter VII - Special Cauliflower Dessert Recipes

This might sound a bit strange but just pay some attention and discover some amazing cauliflower desserts! They are pretty special and delicious!

MMMMMMMMMMMMMMMMMMMMMMMMMMMMMMMM

(61) Cauliflower Rice Pudding

You will forget about regular rice puddings!

Prep Time: 10 minutes

Total Cooking Time: 25 minutes

Serving Size: 4

List of Ingredients:

- ¼ cup raisins
- 1 tsp. cinnamon powder
- 10 stevia drops
- 1 ½ cups almond milk
- 2 cups cauliflower, riced

MMMMMMMMMMMMMMMMMMMMMMMMMMMMMMMMMMM

Instructions:

1. In a pot, mix cauliflower with milk, stevia, cinnamon and raisins, stir and cook over medium heat for 15 minutes.

2. Divide into bowls and serve cold.

Enjoy!

(62) Chocolate Cauliflower Power Bars

These are truly special and tasty!

Prep Time: 10 minutes

Total Cooking Time: 40 minutes

Servings: 8

List of Ingredients:

- 2 cups cauliflower florets, steamed and blended
- 1 cup walnuts, chopped
- 2 Tbsp. coconut oil
- ¼ cup cocoa powder
- ½ cup buckwheat flour
- 1 Tbsp. flaxseed, ground
- ⅓ cup coconut sugar
- 1 Tbsp. chocolate, chopped
- 1 tsp. cinnamon powder

MMMMMMMMMMMMMMMMMMMMMMMMMMMMMMMMM

Instructions:

1. Put cauliflower in a bowl, add oil and stir well.

2. Add walnuts, cocoa, flour, flaxseeds, sugar, cinnamon and chocolate and stir well.

3. Pour everything in a lined baking sheet, spread well, introduce in the oven 350°F and bake for 30 minutes.

4. Lave mix to cool down a bit, cut into 16 bars and serve.

Enjoy!

(63) Special Cauliflower Cake

This is perfect for a special party!

Prep Time: 10 minutes

Total Cooking Time: 45 minutes

Serving Size: 12

List of Ingredients:

- ½ pound cauliflower florets, steamed
- 1 Tbsp. vanilla extract
- ¾ cup vanilla almond milk
- 3 Tbsp. hazelnut oil
- ⅓ cup brown sugar
- ¼ cup cocoa powder
- 3 ounces bittersweet chocolate
- ½ tsp. baking soda
- ¾ cup whole wheat flour
- 1 tsp. baking powder

MMMMMMMMMMMMMMMMMMMMMMMMMMMMMMMMMMMMM

Instructions:

1. In your blender, mix cauliflower with vanilla, milk, oil, sugar, cocoa powder, chocolate, baking soda, baking powder and flour, whisk really well and pour into a greased baking pan.

2. Introduce in the oven at 350°F and bake for 35 minutes.

3. Slice cake and serve.

Enjoy!

(64) Cauliflower Brownies

You really have to try these brownies!

Prep Time: 10 minutes

Total Cooking Time: 40 minutes

Serving Size: 4

List of Ingredients:

- 1 cup cauliflower, steamed and pureed
- ⅓ cup flax meal, ground
- ½ cup cocoa powder
- 1 Tbsp. maple syrup

MMMMMMMMMMMMMMMMMMMMMMMMMMMMMMMMMMM

Instructions:

1. In a bowl, mix cauliflower with flax meal, cocoa powder and maple syrup, stir really well and pour the batter in a baking dish.

2. Bake in the oven at 350°F for 30 minutes, leave brownies aside to cool down, slice and serve them.

Enjoy!

(65) Sweet Cauliflower Dip

Serve this with some strawberries on the side and enjoy!

Prep Time: 30 minutes

Total Cooking Time: 30 minutes

Serving Size: 5

List of Ingredients:

- 1 ¾ cups cauliflower florets, steamed
- 2 Tbsp. cocoa butter, melted
- 5 Tbsp. maple syrup
- 1 Tbsp. almond milk
- ½ tsp. cinnamon powder
- 1 tsp. lemon juice
- 1 tsp. vanilla extract

MMMMMMMMMMMMMMMMMMMMMMMMMMMMMMMMMM

Instructions:

1. In your blender, mix cauliflower with cocoa butter, maple syrup, almond milk, cinnamon, lemon juice and vanilla extract, pulse well, divide into bowls and keep in the fridge for 30 minutes before serving.

Enjoy!

(66) Tasty Cauliflower Cake

This lemony cake is absolutely insane!

Prep Time: 5 hours and 10 minutes

Total Cooking Time: 5 hours and 10 minutes

Serving Size: 6

List of Ingredients:

For the crust:

- 1 and ½ cups pumpkin seeds
- 1 Tbsp. maple syrup
- 8 medjool dates, pitted and chopped

For the filling:

- 2 avocados, pitted and peeled
- 2 cups cauliflower florets
- 8 Tbsp. maple syrup
- 1 cup pineapple, chopped
- 6 Tbsp. lemon juice
- ½ tsp. lemon zest, grated
- 1 tsp. vanilla extract
- ¼ cup poppy seeds

MMMMMMMMMMMMMMMMMMMMMMMMMMMMMMMMMM

Instructions:

1. In your blender, mix pumpkin seeds with 1 Tbsp. maple syrup and dates, blend really well and press on the bottom of a cake pan.

2. Clean your blender, add avocados, cauliflower, maple syrup, pineapple, lemon juice, lemon zest, vanilla seeds and poppy seeds and blend really well.

3. Spread this over crust and keep in the fridge for 5 hours before slicing and serving.

Enjoy!

(67) Cauliflower Rice Pudding

This is so yummy and delicious!

Prep Time: 10 minutes

Total Cooking Time: 15 minutes

Serving Size: 6

List of Ingredients:

- 2 cups cauliflower, riced
- ½ cup almond milk
- ½ cup coconut cream
- 1 tsp. cinnamon powder
- 1 egg
- 2 stevia packets
- Chocolate chips for serving

MMMMMMMMMMMMMMMMMMMMMMMMMMMMMMMMMMM

Instructions:

1. In a heat proof bowl, mix cauliflower with almond milk and coconut cream, stir well and heat up in your microwave for 2 minutes.

2. Transfer this to a small pan, heat up over medium heat, add egg, stevia and cinnamon, stir, cook for 4 minutes, take off heat, cool down, divide into cups and serve with chocolate chips sprinkled on top.

Enjoy!

(68) Amazing Cauliflower Cheesecake

This is so fresh and tasty! We guarantee you will love it!

Prep Time: 2 hours

Total Cooking Time: 2 hours

Serving Size: 6

List of Ingredients:

For the crust:

- 1 cup coconut, shredded
- ¾ cup cashews, soaked for 2 hours and drained
- ¼ tsp. sugar
- ¼ cup lemon juice
- 1 Tbsp. butter, melted

For the filling:

- 2 cups cashews, soaked for 2 hours, drained and chopped
- ½ cup butter
- 1 and ½ cusp cauliflower florets, boiled
- 1 cup raspberries
- 1 Tbsp. lemon juice
- 1 tsp. vanilla extract
- ⅓ cup coconut milk
- 1 Tbsp. maple syrup

MMMMMMMMMMMMMMMMMMMMMMMMMMMMMMMMMM

Instructions:

1. In your blender, mix coconut with ¾ cup cashews, ¼ tsp. sugar, ¼ cup lemon juice and 1 Tbsp. butter, blend really well, press on the bottom of a cake pan and keep in the freezer for 30 minutes.

2. Meanwhile, clean your blender, add 2 cups cashews, ½ cup butter, cauliflower, raspberries, lemon juice, vanilla extract, coconut milk and maple syrup and blend well.

3. Spread this over crust and keep cheesecake in the fridge for 1 hour and 30 minutes before serving.

Enjoy!

(69) Cauliflower Pudding

You should really make this today for your kids! They will adore this pudding!

Prep Time: 3 hours and 10 minutes

Total Cooking Time: 3 hours and 10 minutes

Serving Size: 4

List of Ingredients:

- 20 drops stevia
- ½ cup heavy cream
- 1 cauliflower head, florets separated, boiled and pureed
- ¼ cup cocoa powder
- 1 and ½ tsp. gelatin
- 1 and ½ Tbsp. swerve

MMMMMMMMMMMMMMMMMMMMMMMMMMMMMMMMMM

Instructions:

1. In your blender, mix cauliflower with cocoa, stevia, heavy cream, gelatin and swerve, pulse really well and divide into small ramekins.

2. Keep in the fridge for 3 hours before serving.

Enjoy!

(70) Cauliflower Espresso Cake

This is perfect for a hot summer day!

Prep Time: 6 hours and 10 minutes

Total Cooking Time: 6 hours and 10 minutes

Serving Size: 6

List of Ingredients:

For the crust:

- 2 Tbsp. maple syrup
- 2 Tbsp. coconut oil
- 8 medjool dates, pitted and chopped
- 1 and ½ cups pepitas, chopped

For the filling:

- 8 Tbsp. coconut oil, melted
- 4 and ½ cup cauliflower florets, boiled
- 6 Tbsp. almond milk
- 8 Tbsp. maple syrup
- 1 Tbsp. maca powder
- 1 Tbsp. vanilla extract
- 9 Tbsp. cocoa powder
- 1 Tbsp. blackstrap molasses
- ¾ tsp. espresso powder

MMMMMMMMMMMMMMMMMMMMMMMMMMMMMMMMMM

Instructions:

1. In your blender, mix 2 Tbsp. coconut oil with pepitas, dates and 2 Tbsp. maple syrup, pulse really well and press on the bottom of a cake pan.

2. Clean your blender, add 8 Tbsp. coconut oil, cauliflower, almond milk, 8 Tbsp. maple syrup, maca powder, cocoa powder, vanilla extract, blackstrap molasses and espresso powder, pulse well and spread over your crust.

3. Keep in the freezer for 6 hours, slice and serve.

Enjoy!

About the Author

A native of Indianapolis, Indiana, Valeria Ray found her passion for cooking while she was studying English Literature at Oakland City University. She decided to try a cooking course with her friends and the experience changed her forever. She enrolled at the Art Institute of Indiana which offered extensive courses in the culinary Arts. Once Ray dipped her toe in the cooking world, she never looked back.

When Valeria graduated, she worked in French restaurants in the Indianapolis area until she became the head chef at one of the 5-star establishments in the area. Valeria's attention to taste and visual detail caught the eye of a local business person who expressed an interest in publishing her recipes. Valeria began her secondary career authoring cookbooks and e-books which she tackled with as much talent and gusto as her first career. Her passion for food leaps off the page of her books which have colourful anecdotes and stunning pictures of dishes she has prepared herself.

Valeria Ray lives in Indianapolis with her husband of 15 years, Tom, her daughter, Isobel and their loveable Golden Retriever, Goldy. Valeria enjoys cooking special dishes in her large, comfortable kitchen where the family gets involved in preparing meals. This successful, dynamic chef is an inspiration to culinary students and novice cooks everywhere.

••••••••• ● ● ● ● ●•••••••

Author's Afterthoughts

Thank you for Purchasing my book and taking the time to read it from front to back. I am always grateful when a reader chooses my work and I hope you enjoyed it!

With the vast selection available online, I am touched that you chose to be purchasing my work and take valuable time out of your life to read it. My hope is that you feel you made the right decision.

I very much would like to know what you thought of the book. Please take the time to write an honest and informative review on Amazon.com. Your experience and opinions will be of great benefit to me and those readers looking to make an informed choice.

With much thanks,

Valeria Ray

Made in the USA
Las Vegas, NV
28 February 2023

68302699R00121